SMART BRAIN RIGHT BRAIN

An Introduction to Environmental Engineering

Om KIDZ
An imprint of Om Books International

First Published in 2021 by

Om Kidz | Om Books International

Corporate & Editorial Office
A-12, Sector 64, Noida 201 301
Uttar Pradesh, India
Phone: +91 120 477 4100
Email: editorial@ombooks.com
Website: www.ombooksinternational.com

Sales Office
107, Ansari Road, Darya Ganj
New Delhi 110 002, India
Phone: +91 11 4000 9000
Email: sales@ombooks.com

Author: Shweta Sinha
Editor: Kirti Pathak
Art & Design: Anshuman Pandey, Gaurav Bhandari, Harish Arya

ISBN: 978-93-5276-843-1

Printed in India

10 9 8 7 6 5 4 3 2 1

CONTENTS

1. Our Environment 4
2. Water Pollution 8
3. Air Pollution 13
4. Soil Pollution 18
5. Noise Pollution 23

Let's Get Active 28

Glossary 32

Answer 32

1. Our Environment

We live on a planet called Earth. The Earth is our world. The Earth provides us with all the things we need to live. This is our environment.

Water

Air

Food

Shelter

DID YOU KNOW?

Things that are not built by people are called natural things.

Humans are the cleverest of all beings. They have learnt how to use Earth's resources. They till the land to grow the food they require. They have built cities, roads and bridges. They have built industries to produce better products for themselves.
Things that people build or manufacture are called manmade things. Here are some manmade things:

Buildings

Bridge

Modes of transport

POCKET FACT

Our environment is a mix of manmade and natural things.

Changing Earth

Earth has been around for billions of years. It has seen many changes. But today, our planet is in deep trouble. To make their lives more comfortable, humans have done things that is changing the environment way too quickly. These changes are turning our Earth unhealthy for everyone.

DID YOU KNOW?

About 600 million years ago, Earth was so cold that it was completely covered with ice.

Planet Earth cannot protect itself from humans. It is our job to preserve the wonderful natural resources. It is a good sign that humans are learning to be careful so that their activities do not harm the environment.

POCKET FACT

Greta Thunberg is a young environmental activist. She has been motivating people and governments to stop doing things that hurt the environment.

2. Water Pollution

The freshwater we use at homes comes from a river, a lake or from groundwater. Imagine if one day you find brown water flowing out of your taps. Would you use that dirty water? No, you would not! We cannot use dirty water for drinking, cooking, or anything else because it is harmful for health. You may fall sick if you consume polluted water.

DID YOU KNOW?

We cannot live without drinking water for more than 2-3 days.

How does water get dirty?

Water gets dirty when we throw pollutants in the water body. Pollutants can be chemicals, trash, sewage, etc. Pollutants come from homes, factories and farms. When water becomes dirty, it is called **water pollution**.

POCKET FACT

Soap from washing your car can run down the street drain and cause water pollution.

Picking up trash

Water gets polluted when we throw trash in it. People are now building machines to pick out this trash.

Mr. Trash Wheel

This floating device is a litter gobbling machine.

3. Air Pollution

Air is what we breathe in. Earth is covered by a blanket of air. We call it the atmosphere.

Air is a mixture of many different kinds of gases. Oxygen is one of the gases in the air. We need oxygen to live.

POCKET FACT

Our body takes in oxygen and gives out carbon dioxide gas. Plants take in carbon dioxide and give out oxygen.

When unwanted gases or particles are added to air, it causes air pollution. Things that pollute air are called pollutants. Air pollution causes our eyes to burn and makes it difficult to breathe. It can even make people fall sick.

DID YOU KNOW? Air pollution is making the world a hotter place to live in.

Where does air pollution come from?

There are four main sources that cause air pollution:

Fumes from vehicles such as cars, buses, trucks, aeroplanes and trains

Smoke from factories

Burning wood, trash and other things

Smoke from forest fire

Dust and smoke from wildfires, volcanoes, etc.

POCKET FACT

When some farm animals belch or pass gas, they let out a gas that adds to air pollution.

Keeping the Air clean

The most basic solution to cleaner air is to avoid burning fossil fuels. Fossil fuels include petrol, diesel, coal, etc.

Electric vehicles don't burn fuels like petrol or diesel They run on electricity stored in batteries. So, they don't let out fumes.

Less fumes = Less air pollution

Electric vehicles are almost silent. They help reduce the traffic noise.

Electric car

Electric train

A solar powered aeroplane uses the power of the Sun

DID YOU KNOW? A bicycle does not burn any fuel. It is the most eco-friendly mode of transport.

Electricity generation in thermal power plants burn coal. Burning coal causes air pollution. Newer technology use eco-friendly sources such as the sun, wind, water, etc., to generate electricity.

POCKET FACT

Producing clean energy is important. But equally important is to reduce our usage of electricity.

4. Soil Pollution

Soil lies underneath grass and plants.

Remember to wash the soil from your hands before you eat

Playing with soil is fun, but don't bring it home!

POCKET FACT

Soil is one of Earth's most important natural resources.

How does soil get polluted?

Soil may itself look dirty. Yet, it too can get polluted. Unwanted and toxic materials in soil lead to soil pollution. Here are some things that damage the soil:

DID YOU KNOW? Soil pollution affects the health of plants growing in them. Consuming such plants can make us fall sick.

Sources of Soil Pollution

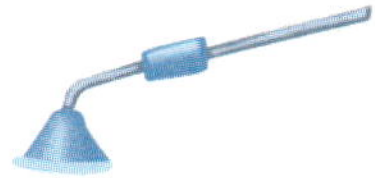

Trash from our homes ends up in landfills. It is buried under the soil. This means all our trash seeps into the soil.

Pesticides and fertilisers are chemicals used in farming. They get absorbed in the farm soil and damage it.

Mining creates large holes in the ground. It also releases toxic chemicals into the soil.

Harmful chemicals and wastewater from factories pollute the soil if they are directly dumped.

POCKET FACT

Pollutants from soil can seep into groundwater and lead to water pollution.

Making Soil less dirty

There are ways to treat polluted soil.

We can dig up the polluted soil and take it away to a disposal site. This is done where a small patch of soil is polluted.

Another way is to heat the soil. Heat turns the chemicals in soil into gas. The gas escapes from the soil. This gas is then safely collected above the ground to prevent air pollution.

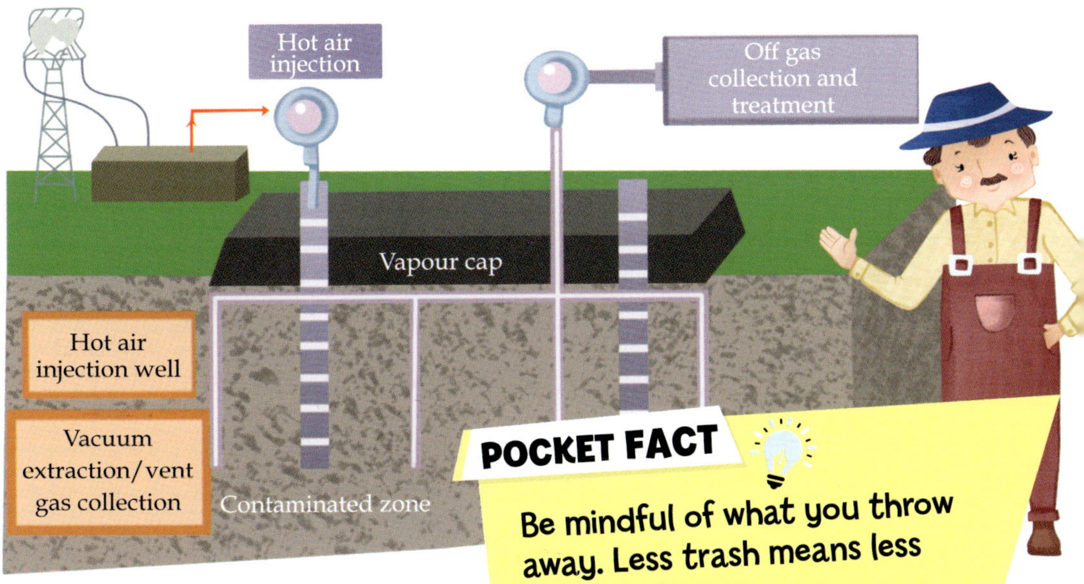

POCKET FACT

Be mindful of what you throw away. Less trash means less soil pollution.

Natural methods

Really tiny living organisms called bacteria are added to the soil.

The bacteria eat up all the extra waste in the soil.

The bacteria digest the waste and turn it into water and harmless gases.

The bacteria release the water that then mixes with the soil.

POCKET FACT

Certain trees and plants also help in absorbing the pollutants from the soil.

5. Noise Pollution

Sound is a part of our daily lives. We make sounds when we talk. But when a sound becomes too loud, it turns into noise. And noise is not pleasant at all.

Noise is produced by traffic, jet planes and helicopters, loudspeakers, factories, and even household gadgets.

DID YOU KNOW? A scientific instrument called a sound level meter is used to measure noise.

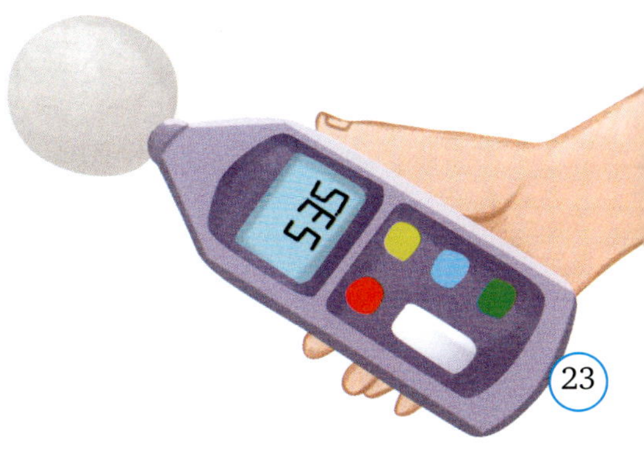

Bad effects of Noise

Not all noise causes noise pollution. If it does not happen regularly, the noise is simply a 'nuisance'. But when noise is so much that it disrupts our daily life, it turns into noise pollution.

Noise pollution disturbs our sleep. It makes us anxious and irritable. Too much noise even damages our hearing.

POCKET FACT

Sound is measured in decibels(dB). The sound of rustling leaves is 20-30 dB, while that of a thunderclap is 120 dB.

Noise affects not just people, but animals too. Excessive noise by ships and submarines are hurting and killing the whales. Animals use sounds to communicate with each other. Noise pollution makes it difficult for them to do so.

DID YOU KNOW?

Sounds that reach 85dB or more can harm a person's ears.

Noise Insulation

In industries, noisy machines are kept in soundproof rooms. The walls of a soundproof room are made of materials that absorb sound. That way the noise stays inside the room.
Sound proofing is also done in theatres so that their sounds do not go outside.

DID YOU KNOW?

Airports and industries are built far away from residential areas. This prevents the noise from affecting the people living there.

Electric train

Electric vehicles are almost silent. They help to reduce traffic noise.

Electric car

Construction workers wear noise cancelling headphones. This protects their ears from the noise.

DID YOU KNOW?

Trees help in absorbing sound too. Planting trees along roads and in residential areas is a good way to reduce noise pollution.

Let's Get Active

Manmade or Natural

Circle all the manmade things below.

Sources of Pollution

What kind of environmental pollution is happening in these pictures? Write 'W' for water, 'A' for air, 'S' for soil and 'N' for Noise.

Label each step in wastewater treatment. Choose labels from the box below:

Screens	Treatment Centre	Primary Settlement Tanks
River	Aeration Chamber	Secondary Settlement Tanks